Peace, Love and War

Dave Puller

© Dave Puller 2010
Peace, Love and War

ISBN 978-0-9567733-0-2

Published by
PULLER PUBLICATIONS
58 Orchard Road West
Northenden
Manchester
M22 4ED

A CIP catalogue record of this book
can be obtained from the British Library.

Book designed by Michael Walsh at
THE BETTER BOOK COMPANY
5 Lime Close, Chichester PO19 6SW
Printed by
IMPRINTDIGITAL.NET
Seychelles Farm, Upton Pyne, Exeter Devon EX5 5HY

Contents

This book is dedicated to all the people I love, those who are living, and those who are not. Thanks for making my life special.

Introduction

Poets and priests have much in common. For both, words are not just important, they are essential tools of the trade: words are all we have in our attempt to name our experiences, hopes and beliefs. In a special memorial service at St. Anne's, remembering those who have died in our city, the vulnerable, the homeless, those struggling with addiction, Dave's poems' have played an important part. The unmistakeable and often uncompromising directness of his words always make an impact.

The "ouch" factor, is still present in this new volume of work, as is a distinctive wry wit, which meant that whilst reading these poems I found myself either smiling or wincing, or doing both at the same time. This is especially true of the poems written in reaction to war, which are, perhaps, the strongest and most passionate in this collection. I found the poem "By the banks of the Euphrates" especially poignant.

But what I like best is the questioning nature of some of Dave's poetry. Questions are at the heart of things, they are a challenge, a provocation, an invitation to pause and reflect, an opportunity to look more closely at the world in which we live, and consider how it might become a better world.
Which is where Love comes in.

As I said, poets and priests have much in common.

Gisela Raines

Associate Rector
St. Anne's Church
Manchester.

About the Author

Dave Puller was born in Manchester in 1951, under the name of Dave Wraxall. He has lived in Wythenshawe all of his life. After leaving school at the age of fifteen, with no qualifications, he had a succession of jobs, including, junior soldier, stock exchange clerk, factory worker, window cleaner, professional boxer, salesman and teacher.

Dave is now a professional poet, writer and performer and is a genuine, innovative and original talent, emerging from the early days of the alternative comedy scene in Manchester. He is founder of the long running satirical shows *How many days 'til Xmas* and *What the papers said*. He is the author of several stage plays and has also written for radio, television and film.

He regularly performs in Manchester and around the country touring with his show *Dave Puller's Upside Down World*. He works at prisons, schools and community venues and encourages people to write about their life experiences, and if possible, to perform their work.

This is Dave's third collection of poetry and he would like to thank Barbara, Cher, and Kristian for putting up with his years of ranting and raving, for sticking by him when things have gone wrong and for the support they constantly give him. He does appreciate that support.

He would also like to thank friends Claire Mooney, Steve O'Donoghue and Tony Sides. They have worked with him for many years on the satirical shows he writes, often without money, or an audience, and have never once complained. They are true professionals and friends.

Special thanks to Michael Walsh, as without his help and encouragement, this book would not have been produced. Thanks Pete.

Dave hopes this book makes you laugh, cry, and leaves you thinking about how we can all make the world a better place.

Let's Have a Revolution for Fun

This poem was inspired by a work by D H Lawrence.

Let's have a revolution
Without violence or malice
Let's have the launch at
Buckingham Palace
Let's have politicians
Eating clichés and lies
Invade their hypocrisies
With soft custard pies
Let's have no borders
That keeps poor people away
Let's have "You are welcome" signs
"We hope you will stay"

Let's stop making warplanes
Tanks and Guns
Teach humanity
To our
Daughters and Sons
Let age old enemies
Turn a new page
Let Love and Kindness
Replace
Hate and Rage

Let everyone share
In the wealth that's made

Let's have a regular
Happy Parade

Let's have a revolution
For all to share
Let's have a revolution
To show we all care
Let's have a revolution
Without violence or
Malice
Let's have the launch at
Buckingham Palace.

Who Knows Where Our Time Goes?

This poem was inspired by a Sandy Denny song. She died in 1972. The words of the song were haunting. If you haven't heard the song I suggest you do so. It may make you think about the direction of your life.

Who knows where our time goes
What happened to our
Highs
Our lows
Our dreams

Our schemes
Our good times
Our bad times
Our yesterdays
Our tomorrows
Our happiness
Our sorrows
Our beginnings
Our ends
Our enemies
Our friends
Our smiles
Our tears
Our months
Our years

Who knows where our time
Goes
Only
Us.

The Mobile Phone

Got to use the mobile phone
Walking down the street
Got to use the mobile phone
Think I'm cool
I'm sweet

Got to drink that smart
New beer
Bottle in one hand
Phone to my ear

Got to visit
Trendy bars
Got to drive the
Fastest cars
Got to wear designer gear
With that phone
Pressed to my ear

Got to think I'm
Mister Big
Got to smoke that expensive
Cig

Got to use
The mobile phone
Even when
I'm all alone

Even when
I'm all alone
Hello
Hello
Is there anybody there?
Is there anybody there?

The Company Rebel

He
Wanted
To
Be
The
Company
Rebel

But
Corporate
Policy
Would
Not
Allow
It.

Has Anyone Ever

Has anyone ever read Anthem for Doomed Youth
Has anyone ever heard an MP tell the truth
Has anyone fell in love with a friend
Has anyone ever wanted a relationship to end

Has anyone ever got drunk and felt a fool
Has anyone ever peed in a public swimming pool
Has anyone ever stole toffees from the shops
Has anyone ever climbed the shelters at bus stops

Has anyone been scared by the challenges of life
Has anyone any woman ever thought they were just
A mother or a wife
Has anyone ever been afraid of emotions or a touch
Has anyone ever told their family they love them very much

Has anyone ever hid from a the knock on the door
Has anyone ever had enough yet still wanted more
Has anyone ever heard of a Ministry of Offence
Has anyone ever thought that war makes no sense

Has anyone ever called someone they don't know a mate
Has anyone ever said they like someone they really hate
Has anyone ever had to pawn their wedding rings
Has any of you ever done any of these things.

Domestic Violence

Twelve o'clock on a Saturday night
The time approaches
For a drunken fight
The bedroom dark and full of
Silence
Time once more for some
Domestic violence

Voices raised
The point is near
Hid under blankets
Surrounded by fear

Punches thrown
Screams of pain
Kicks to the body
More punches rain

The head banging
Against the wall
More punches
More screams
Then to the floor
She'll fall

The bedroom dark and full of
Silence
The time has passed
For
Domestic Violence.

The World

I wanted some tiles
So I went to
Tile World

I wanted some wallpaper
So I went to
Paper World

I wanted some furniture
So I went to
Furniture World

I want a
Better World
Where will I go?

Middle England United

Good old middle England
With its village green
Cricket on a Sunday
Beef that's good and lean

Good old middle England
The little semi-detached
The off-road vehicle
With towing bar attached

Good old middle England
The private pension plan
Tax relief encompassed
Gives you all it can

Good old middle England
Kids in private school
Charitable status for everyone
They are no-one's fool

Good old middle England
Where troubles always pass
It's good old middle England
And fuck the
Working Class.

Posh Kids

Waiting
At
The
Bus
Stop

The
Posh
Kids

In
Their
Posh
Uniforms

Being
Taken
To
Their
Posh
School

On
Their
Free
Bus

Courtesy
Of
The
Poor.

My Geography Teacher

Mr. Kellett was my
Geography teacher
He hated me
I hated him

Four years of
Hell
For both of
Us.

Diffident

I always thought you rather
Diffident, he commented

I disagreed
With him

Telling him

I
Just
Lacked
A
Little
Self-assurance.

Come To Sellafield

I wrote this poem after hearing a radio commercial asking me to visit Sellafield nuclear re-processing plant. Apparently it is a great day out and is very safe. Really.

Come to Sellafield
It's a great day out
You can feel
You can touch
You can mess about

Come to Sellafield
Have some fun
You can watch
Our plutonium production run

Come to Sellafield
See the Dead Sea
There's lots to do
For you and me

Come to Sellafield
It's such a great sight
We've got
Sheep and Pigs
That glow at night
Come to Sellafield
It's really a must

We'll show you a local
Cancer cluster

Come to Sellafield
It's Hyperactive
It's Interactive
It's Superactive
And hey, it's
RADIOACTIVE.

Children In Need

There were wannabe celebrities
Grade three stars
Telling stories
To tug at our hearts

There were children to clothe
Mouths to feed
Yet nobody asked why
There were
Children in Need

There was Terry Wogan
Smiling away

Jimmy Tarbuck
Offering himself for a day

There were children to clothe
Hungry mouths to feed
Still nobody asked why
There were
Children in Need

No
Nobody asked
Why
There
Were
Children
In
Need.

I understand the first radio broadcast for children in need
took place in 1928. It is the year 2008 and there are still
children in need.

Charity

We give to this
Donate to that
We put our money
In the bucket and hat

We run for MIND
Walk for scope
We pull double-deckers
With a nylon rope

We have fancy dress
Sponsored swims
We have nights of silence
Community slims

We have Red Nose Day
Children in Need
Presented by celebrities
Whose motto is greed

We give to charity
To cleanse our soul
But charity will never question
It will only console.

Ibiza Holiday

I'm here on holiday
On the Island of Ibiza
I'll have
Egg and Bacon
For breakfast
And for tea
I'll have
Chips and Pizza

I'll wash it all down
With ten pints
Of beer
I'm on the island of
Ibiza
I love
Being
Here.

We

We've been ruled
We've been fooled
We've been preached at
We've been screeched at
We've been drilled
We've been killed

We've been stacked
We've been sacked
We've been sticked
We've been kicked
We've been whipped
We've been shipped

We've been patronized
We've been criminalized
We've been socialized
We've been demonized
We've been bowed
We've been cowed

We've been taught to crawl
We've been taught to brawl
We've been taught to run
We've been working class
What utter fun.

Gas Lighters

On Altrincham market
They were five for a pound

On Wythenshawe market
They were three for a pound

Funny
But on reflection
And considering the socio-economic variants
Of the respective areas
I thought it would have
Been the other way round.

Visit to an NHS Hospital Private Unit

As I entered I was greeted by a pleasant
Smiling receptionist
'Who have you come to visit?' she enquired.
I gave her the name of my friend
Her suite is number nine
On the right
Down the corridor, she informed me

She offered tea, coffee, biscuits and the
Morning papers
I accepted tea and biscuits
There was, she said, a small private lounge available
Complete with radio and television, if I needed it

My visit lasted about one hour
We talked about pasts, about futures
It ended with a kiss, a hug and a tear
An unspoken confirmation of the love
Between us

As I left
I noticed a poster, which said
This facility is run by BUPA
In partnership with the NHS
We hope you have enjoyed
Your visit

I left with
Warm
Loving
Thoughts
Of
My
Dying
Friend.

The Park

In the dark
The swings silent
No one climbing
The frame

The horse at rest
The slide empty
Nobody flying
The witches' hat

The park deserted
Except
For you
For me

In the shelter
Kissing
Touching
Fondling

Hopefully
Going
All
The
Way.

Childhood Romance

I was really upset
When
She
Chucked
Me

So sad and
Downhearted
Could not believe
She'd finished with me
Could not believe
We'd parted

I couldn't eat
I couldn't sleep
Didn't know what to do

But five minutes later
You came along
And now
I really
Love you.

Wish

She
Gave
Me
Her
Heart

I
Gave
It
Back

Wish
I'd
Kept
It.

Memory

There's no memory
As strong
Or
As vivid
As
A
False
One
Especially
A
False
One.

Old Enough

I could have loved you
If I had been a lot younger

We could gone walking
Along Morecambe Promenade

Posed by the statue of
Eric Morecambe

Visited Southport or Rhyl
Climbed the Great Orme at Llandudno

Walked the wall of Chester
Ambled along Blackpool Pier

We could have done all those things
If I had been a lot younger

Or
If you had been a lot
Older.

Misunderstanding

She didn't understand
The protocols
Of the
I Love You words

When I said the words
I Love You
I expected her to say
 I Love You back

But when I said
I Love You

She just looked at
Me and said
Me too.

Love Trilogy

Coming as it did
Abruptly
Quickly
Cruelly
It was a bit
Of a shock
But I should have
Seen the signs
For they were there
When you stopped
Kissing me
When you stopped
Making love to me
When you moved into
The spare bedroom
And when you stopped
Talking to me
The signs were there
Alright
But I didn't see them
They do say
Love is blind.

When you left me
You took
My heart
You took
My soul

Then you came back
And
Took everything else.

After you'd finished
With me
You said we could
Still be friends
That was nine
Years ago
And we
Haven't spoken
since.

Late Lunch, Part One

She'd made lunch
Butter on the bread
Brown bread of course
Healthier
Corned beef and salad
She also brought along
Some cherry tomatoes
Hard and juicy
I couldn't eat the
Corned beef

I didn't have the heart
To tell I was a
Vegetarian
Or that I didn't like
Brown bread
So I slid the meat off
When she wasn't looking
And I ate the
The brown bread
I'd waited twenty five years for
This lunch
Corned beef butties
On brown bread
Salad
Cherry tomatoes
And her
The things you do
For love.

Assertiveness

I wanted
To be
More
Assertive
But
You
Wouldn't
Allow
It.

Tunnel of Love

This poem came about after a trip to Blackpool with the local youth club. I was fourteen at the time.

That day in
The tunnel of Love
She kissed me to
Perfection
That day in
The Tunnel of Love
She
eased my juvenile erection
That day in
The Tunnel of Love
In the warm
Blackpool weather
That day in
The Tunnel of Love
We rocked our bodies
Together
That day in
The Tunnel of Love
For evermore
That day in
The Tunnel of Love
Two poor kids
From Wythenshawe.

When The Lights Go Out

This poem was written after I heard a conversation, on the radio, with a member of a band called The Scissor Sisters.

When you turn the lights out
Think of me
Think of the things
You can't touch or see
Think of the things you
Didn't say
Think of the things
You did that day
Think of the things
You could have done
Think of what
You could have won
So when you turn the
Lights out
And you can't see
Close your eyes
And think of me
Close your eyes
Then you can see
What you're missing
When you're
Missing me.

Always on My Mind

I think of you
When I'm driving
I think of you
When I'm walking
I think of you
When I'm working
I think of you
When I'm shopping
I think of you
When I'm reading
I think of you
When I'm watching TV
I dream of you
When I'm sleeping
You are always
On my mind.

Problem

It's
The
Thoughts
Of
You
That
Cause
The
Problem
The
Problem
Is
They
Are
Only
Thoughts.

School Reunion

I'd loved her
For thirty years or more
I'd tell her as
Soon
As
I
Walked through
The door
I wanted to ask
Her
If she felt
The same
But the
Trouble was
I
Couldn't
Remember
Her
Name.

Poetic Combination

You ask me
What is
Poetry

You
Look into my
Eyes
And ask

What is
Poetry

To
Me

Poetry
Is
You

You ask me
What is
Love

You
Look into my
Eyes
And ask

What is
Love

To
Me

Love
Is
You

Poetry
Love
You
The
Perfect
Combination.

Everything

I gave her
Everything
And
She took it.

It's Best Not To Bother

She stopped kissing
She thought it would
Give her wrinkles

She stopped having sex
She thought it was
Too much
Like hard work

She stopped loving
She thought
It was easier
Not to
Bother.

Want

I wanted to talk about revolution
She wanted me to hoover

I wanted to rant about politics
She wanted clean the bathroom

I wanted to discuss philosophy
She wanted me to cut the grass

I wanted to go on a demonstration
She wanted to go to B & Q

I wanted to make love
She wanted to read

Two wants
Neither satisfied.

Friendship

Now that we are friends
After all these years
We can share
Each other's laughter
Calm each others fears

We can tell each other thoughts
Which have
Remained inside
Our heads
Talk about things
We never would
Have said

We can touch each other's
Hearts
Dry each other's
Tears
Now that we are
Friends
After all
These years.

Two Lovers

I Love you
He said
I love you too
She replied.

No More

No more
Making love
On the living room floor
No more
Seeing your face
As you walk through
The door

No more fights
Over what's on TV
For there's
No more you
There's
No more me

No more reasons
For falling out
No more reasons
To scream and
Shout

No more
To do
No more
To see

For there's
No more
You
There's
No more
Me.

Nothing

There's nothing
Between us
But ourselves
The love has been hidden
By the blindness
In our eyes

There's nothing between us
But ourselves

You
Me
And the
Emptiness

I Have a Dream

This poem is dedicated to a Miss Daisy Speedwell, who was locked up for forty years, for being happy when she was a child. She used to whistle and sing tunes as a young girl. People thought she was mad, so she was put into a mental institution. When she was released forty years later she was still happy, but slightly bitter. She said all she wanted to do was make people happy and full of love.

I have a dream
I believe in love
Love is all you need
I'm going to tape
My favourite love songs
Send them to
Leaders of the world
Make them listen to
This old heart of mine
Join the caravan of love
Get on board the love train
Tell them
Love is in the air
Of the Power of love
The eternal flame
The glory of love
Ask them to
Unchain the melody
Be for real

Love the fascist
Love the racist
Love the bigot
Love the enemy
Love the neighbour
I have a dream
Love is all you need
Love is all you need
Love is all you need.

Quick Date

As I
Arrived
She
Left.

You

You
Picked me up
When
I was down
Made me smile
When
I could only
Frown
You held my
Heart
So it could mend
Then you
Pissed off
With
My
Best
Friend.

Tonight

Tonight
I can see you

Tonight
I can touch you

Tonight
I can hold you

Tonight
I can kiss you

Tonight
I can make love to you

For
Tonight
I can dream.

Heart

You say
You have a
Heart
A genuine beating
Heart

What you
Possess
Is not a
Heart

It is a
Machine
That in time
With a moment

Makes a noise
But
Feels
Nothing.

The Perfect Politician

In order to gain
Peace
He
Went
To
War
In order to protect
Lives
He
Killed
People
In order to save the
Country
He
Destroyed
It
In order to hide the
Truth
He
Told
Lies
He was indeed
The
Perfect
Politician

Poem for Jean

I wrote this poem in memory of Jean McConville, a mother of ten children, who was taken by the IRA after helping an injured and dying British soldier.

They came in
Number
Eighteen of them
Four Women
Fourteen Men
For one Woman
A mighty Woman
For Jean
They were neighbours
Friends
Comrades in
Catholicism
Brit haters
Unforgiving
Giving
Jean
The bullets of
Righteousness
Jean the
Mother
Jean
Full of Love
Full of Compassion
Full of Humanity

Jean
An example
To them
All.

Gods

They spoke to
Their Gods

Their Gods
Spoke back

Invoking them
To kill

It's odd that a God
Would do that

But as they say
Round our way

There's
Nowt
So
Strange
As
Gods

Bombs r Us

We've got
Big bombs
Little bombs
Small bombs
Tiny bombs
Mini bombs
Thin bombs
Fat bombs
Dumb bombs
Quiet bombs
Silent bombs
Cluster bombs
Round bombs
Square bombs
Long bombs
Short bombs
Flat bombs
Cheap bombs
Dear bombs
Lots of bombs
You want some?

You're going
To
Get
Some.

Star-Crossed Lovers

One day, a few years ago, during the time of the Balkans war, I was listening to the radio when the DJ made a flippant remark about the war there. A couple of young lovers were promised safe passage out of their besieged town, so that they could be married. As they left their building and reached open ground they were murdered by a sniper. The DJ then played the Hot Chocolate record Everyone's a Winner.

Everyone's a winner
Said the words on the
Old record
And the butcher smiled
From ear to ear
As he put another
Victim to the
Sword
It's all, all or nothing
At all
As another innocent
Begins to fall
I'm gonna
Tell you how it's gonna be
A little for you
Most of it for
Me

He ain't heavy
He's my brother
She lay murdered
By her lover
It's just
Another lovely day
As a couple of lovers
Just fade away
As
A
Couple
Of
Lovers
Just
Fade
Away.

No September Tears

No eulogies for
These dead
No moments of
Silence
No honourable place
In history

No everlasting memory
No world changing
Order
No
Last Post
No
Going Down
With the Sun

For these were
The dead of
Chile
Of
Allende

The forgotten
No September flowers
No September flags
No September tears.

By the Banks of The Euphrates

By the banks of the Euphrates
He lay
His arms outstretched
As if pleading
To his unseen God

She was nearby
Stilled by the gunfire
Almost close enough
To touch

Almost
But not quite

As the bullets of
Liberation
Flew over their
Heads
She injured
He Dead

There they
Lay
By the banks of
The Euphrates
Mesopotamia
Both
Liberated.

The Good Guys

It's alright for the good guys
To kill children in their sleep

It's alright for the good guys
To make mothers and fathers weep

It's alright for the good guys
To kill and burn and maim

It's alright for the good guys
To mock those who complain

It's alright for the good guys
To use weapons as if they are toys

It's alright for the god guys
To rip arms off little boys

It's alright for the good guys
To bomb a market place

It's alright for the good guys
To show a two-sided face

It's alright for the good guys
To torture, kill and lie

It's alright for the good guys
To watch the innocents die

It's alright for the good guys
To pretend they really care

It's alright for the good guys
To whoop and cheer with glee

It's alright for the good guys
Whoever they may be.

Qana
(MK-84 Guided Bomb BSU-37-B)

Qana
Where Jesus turned
Water into wine
And where
The Israeli
Air Force
Turned
Children
Into
Dust
Courtesy of
The USA
MK-84
Guided Bomb
BSU-37-B.

Commando Tommy and Cowboy Pete

I killed a lot of Germans
When I was a boy
Thought my gun was real
Not just a toy
In my Commando Tommy outfit
I looked really good
I was out to kill
Lusting for blood
I killed Japs too
A bayonet in the belly
I'd seen soldiers do that
In films on the telly

Then the next day
I'd be Cowboy Pete
With my gun and rifle
I was cool
I was sweet
I'd blast Sioux Indians
Shoot them down dead
With their bows and arrows
Skin that was red

As Commando and Cowboy
I was number one
But I'm an adult now

I've no need for a gun
And if I was asked to kill
I know I'd resist
I believe in life
I'm a
Pacifist.

Wythenshawe Anthem

They built the multi-storeys
To house the working class
They gave us lifts
They gave us verandas
But they didn't give us grass

Some of us went to suburbia
A garden city of delight
Where there were pubs and there
Were churches
So we could pray
And we could fight

They gave us infants and primaries
And our junior schools
They gave us
Secondary Moderns
For those of us thought
Fools

They gave us our factories
With our buses to the gate
A number on our clock cards
With jobs we grew to hate

They gave us a
Civic Centre
With it's theatre, bar and baths
Where the middle classes

Could visit
To swim, to drink, to laugh

They gave us flats and houses
With rooms heated by coal
But they forgot to give us identity
They forgot about our soul

They surrounded us with motorways
So people could drive past
They gave us notoriety
A reputation built to last

Then they took away our factories
The buses to the gate
Our hopes ambitions and futures
Consigned to market fate
They told us we were scroungers
Relying on our dole
They took away our self-esteem
They hid away our soul

They built the multi-storeys
To house the working class
They gave us lifts
They gave us verandas
But they didn't give us grass

They put us in suburbia
A garden city of delight
They named our town
Wythenshawe
And hid it out of sight.

Moving House

One day when I arrived home
From school
I thought my family
Had moved house
Without telling me
but they'd left a
Few things behind
there was
The tatty three-piece suite
The old Radiogram
The bed which I shared
With my three brothers
Then I saw my brother
Sid
Coming round the corner
I asked why we'd moved
Don't be daft
Said Sid
We haven't moved anywhere
We've just been
Evicted.

Whose Shoes?

Today it was my brother's
Turn to wear the shoes
He would have to go to school
I could stay at home
He would do three days
This week
I'd do two
I liked it that way
He had bigger feet than me
So I had to put newspaper in them
Pushing it up to the toes
It stopped them curling up
But it didn't stop them looking
Too big for me
Still I didn't have to worry
About that today
I could go back to sleep
And worry about that
Tomorrow.

Rich and Famous

If everyone knew my name
And recognised my face
I'd be rich and famous
I'd stay in expensive hotels
Have homes in
Geneva, Milan, Hollywood
And a mansion in Royal Tunbridge Wells
I'd have six bodyguards, a psychoanalyst and
A personal trainer
If I was rich and famous
I'd eat out in the trendiest places
Be seen with all the best faces
If I was rich and famous
I'd fly around the world in my
Private Jet
To see the poor, needy and hungry
Then surrounded by the press
I'd blame the politicians for
Causing such a mess
And when I'd gone
The poor, needy and hungry would say
That was someone
Rich and Famous
I'd go on chat shows to plug
My latest book
Wear sunglasses in the dark
So people would look and say
There's someone

Rich and famous
I'd pretend to care
About crime, unemployment and the
Homeless
That's what I'd do
I promise you
If I was
Rich and famous.

My Holiday

I wanted to go to
Spain for a holiday
But I couldn't
Afford it
So I hired a
Deckchair
From my local
Hire anything shop
Sat in my back garden
And got soaking
Wet.

The Young Poet

When I started writing poetry
I wrote about
War
Famine
Death and
Hate
I was rather serious
For a boy of
Eight.

You're In For It

Wait until
Your Dad
Comes
Home
My Mum
Used to tell
Me and our kid
Which fortunately
For us
He very Rarely
Did.

Syrup or Honey

When I was young
Our family had no money
We didn't have
Jam, marmalade
Syrup or Honey
We'd have Echo margarine
Thinking it was
Butter
We'd go looking for dropped pennies
In the roadside gutter
On Monday mornings
Mum would send me to look
For someone who'd lend her
Money
On the Family allowance book
On Thursday nights we all had a
Treat
My dad would bring home
Fish and chips
And He let us
Watch him eat
We often had no electric
And sometimes even no gas
It was never pleasant
Being
Lower
Working
Class.

The Clubman

It was almost Christmas
Time for
The Clubman to call
Mum always went into debt
To buy Christmas presents
For us all
Took her all year to
Pay it off
It really was a pain
That took her back to
December
Time to do it all over
Again.

Pleasant Dreams

We could never pay the milkman
Or even afford the rent
Every Tuesday morning
To the pawnbroker I was sent
We'd get a few bob for
My mums wedding rings
It stopped us all starving
We'd get food and other things

I'd get a bottle of mineral
A packet of custard creams
Then I'd go to bed
Quite happy
Wrapped up in
Pleasant dreams.

Mr Hide

Mr Hide
Could mend shoes
I was sent round
When mine developed holes
He looked at me with
His kind warm eyes
Said
I'm sorry son
I can't mend
Plimsoles.

If

This was inspired by the news that Rudyard Kipling's IF had been voted the country's favourite poem.

If Thatcher hadn't been elected
If state education hadn't been neglected
If Britain's miners
Could still dig coal
If New Labour hadn't sold it's soul
If Tony Blair had any ideals
If British Rail hadn't lost its wheels
If industry fat cats weren't so fat
If public services were still just that
If Britain's youth could find a career
If the words
Working Class
Weren't considered a smear
If the NHS wasn't a self-governing trust
If a mobile phone wasn't considered a must
If all single parents didn't get the blame
If things were different
Would they be the same
Life is full of
Ifs
But
What
If
What
If.